Clover Peake
Beasts and Volcanoes

Newton-le-Willows

Published in the United Kingdom in 2019
by The Knives Forks And Spoons Press,
51 Pipit Avenue,
Newton-le-Willows,
Merseyside,
WA12 9RG.

ISBN 978-1-912211-42-5

Copyright © Clover Peake, 2019.

The right of Clover Peake to be identified as the author of this work has been asserted by them in accordance with the Copyrights, Designs and Patents Act of 1988. All rights reserved. No part of this publication may be reproduced, stored in a retrieval system, transmitted in any form or by any means, electronic, photocopying, recording or otherwise, without prior permission of the publisher.

Special thanks to my family and Angie Gillman

Contents

Baby Girl	7
Brother	8
Drunk	9
Etna	10
Etna 2	11
Now That You Are Gone	12
Drink	13
Flesh Trade	14
In The Twilight	16
Message	18
On The Street	19
Encounter	20
She Was Singing It	21
Fentanyl Withdrawal	22
Zennor	27
River Crossing	28
The Blood	30

Baby Girl

The only time I see you now
is when I sleep

I tell the whole story from start to finish
Won't do that anymore

Black and cream anemones cluster in my hands

Their black centres like ox hearts
clots on the butcher's floor

Mud under my nails
from where I was searching
has washed away

Just when I sleep

Brother

The fig tree has been cut down
just starting to bud
It defied sealed rooms
and corridors

The spindle survived winter
doubling its skirts
curtsying to summer

In it was the Peloponnese
towers and goat clangs
or that garden crammed with bird cages
where we sat tearing open fruit

Drunk

Impatient for a greater love
you step into darkness
curl and convulse
to be taken
The thirsty yearning
at peace
at rest
in the long drowning

Etna

Through the clouds we come in
fields are pale
worked
Tied to the bed

The ground is rough but level
Fruits
crops
trees
and flowers
thrive with alchemy

Smoke gathers in the dark
She breathes

watching for those she has lost
Burning in her pit

she pants almost silently

Etna 2

Creating to destroy
the fire in her belly
swallows the young
of those who got greedy

Her shoulders hunch a bit
It's been a long wait
she's held her tongue

Not worried about little mistakes
fighting and stealing
but empty silence
of nights
An unloved eternity

Who is she anymore
body rigid with scars
dust covered necrosis

Not much to say now

Did she just move
Her haunches slid back a little
half lazy
or was it seductive

She can't move much more
She wants her children
Her body is rigid now

It won't be forgiven

Clover Peake

Now That You Are Gone

Now that you're gone
will I forget the moon
Is 28 just a number
carved on bone
Have I unfecunded myself
Do wolves no longer
hear
those
nights
we shared
Is it grey now
Put right

The brilliant mess
at its end
burnt out ravings join the queue
of uncradled heads

There's a hole
in my stomach
Good job
Laparoscopic I see
A tunnel
reaches my gullet
shuttling
vacant cries
from the pit
where mayhem
used to lie

Drink

I'm looking for someone
to paint the walls black with

and the ceiling
and take out the lights

Someone to light a candle
watch shadows fall

on the black walls
watch the shadows

Clover Peake

Flesh Trade

It's 12:30
I fell asleep early
Upstairs
I find you
drenched in TV light
Joe Frazier's face
fills the screen
his story even bigger
Something godly

Earlier you wanted my story
I can't say fully
Just the bits I've said out loud
The bits
practised first
faltering
gauging each reaction

What happens when secrets
meet the air
A flat June air
won't break into a storm
it hangs
fat clouds of unbroken heat

We no longer decide who we are

Joe Frazier worked fields as a boy
drove back scamboogahs
in the school yard

His flesh
his wound
his trade

On the corner of the street
I put down my bag
and call you
Coming in your slippers
you lean in as though for a kiss
but ask where *they* are

Together we walk past a bunch of men

In The Twilight

The pavement carries my soul
to hide in the basements and the fumes
Hold me in your arms
The sun bled into the rooftops long ago

A woman used to walk this hour
barebreasted
Her pockmarked man loves her
He boards up the smashed window panes

There is a woman
she lies
Her child no longer sees her
Jessie loves her

I am in the street
passed the school gates
Plane trees lay down shadows in the playground
Trains shudder behind the houses
They never go anywhere else

The end house where travellers settle
is the last house
In the day they sit on the steps
Children whose milk teeth turn brown

call 999 for fun

I am home here

just renting with everyone else

No one lives here

Everyone has stayed here

on their way to better times

We don't make money

count coppers

put down bottle lids for chips

On Beatrice Rd

shattered car windows

dam up the gutters

diamonds for the girls

with too big handbags

Natasha gets the belt

and Helen steals someone elses pocket money

On a quiet Sunday

when here

was just somewhere to live

Message

A blackbird flew through the canteen window
over the stooped heads of ghosts and orphans
throwing itself against the glass

It searched an exit
a garden

Would a hand snatch it

Someone raised the window

The crockery clattered
bubbles foamed and
custard stewed in vats

On The Street

You said be there
bare chested except the rosary
A ring of lights in the night
capture everything

Barefoot at dawn
daylight crowns the rooftops
lighting the marks of night

The instant surfaces and diminishes
as the eye's pupil twitches

There on the floor
naked
hemmed in by bodies
jeering something

The cacophony freezes
it is all gone

Barefoot in the street
No phone
No keys

Hear the world turning

Encounter

I walk towards
I keep walking
I don't walk away
I did smile
I bluff
I stay straight faced
You mustn't know
I watch
You watch
You're close
I can be closer
I cheat
You miss this
I decide then
I watch you
watching
Your eyes checking
I buy the pretence
I pretend to believe
A pause
eye contact
discerning anything genuine
you shift from one foot to the other
hand in your pocket
Has the door been locked

She Was Singing It

She put it in a song
It was a cry
a warning

But girls
stride
on Perspex

Or a few years back
it was glass

Young women
dance with their wings outstretched
translucent webbing
in headlights

On the train platform snowflakes
circle a girl in a white mini dress

Dawn is hers

Clover Peake

Fentanyl Withdrawal

We're at Moonfleet
A hotel for families
on the Fleet Lagoon
a bank of water
where Chesil Beach
splits from earth itself

I'm with my son
my boyfriend
and his son
I'm unnaturally content
at peace
as though it's game over
I explain to the boys
that in the country
or by the sea
I am myself
I recognise myself
and what matters most

We have dinner
talking for the first time
over a meal
for the first time
in months
The boys are watching a film
in *The Ballroom*
and
we would've loved a baby together
we sort of felt it wasn't allowed

Then we all go upstairs
for all my whole-hearted contentment
there's a fucking shadow
it's so dark
I'm scared to look
I see pain
in every single interaction
I see into that kernel
of pain in all of us
the bit where life tore open our hearts
spat acid on the wound
let it heal
then did the same again
but worse

It's that place in all of us
that makes us bad
and it's all I see
I'm pretending
it's fucking lovely
and this isn't happening
in the middle of a family holiday

I see it when my stepson refuses to be kind to my son
that
he feels unloveable
The wound in my son
makes him repeatedly chase acceptance from his stepbrother
and how fucking rare acceptance ever truly is
The hurt-chain keeps
forming new links

Clover Peake

I want to snap it
but I'm watching
all this
in bliss

Later at bedtime
I feel nausea
in the bathroom
with the huge
brass-footed bath
in the centre of the black and white tiles
I am sick everywhere
in front of the boys
R___ stares
B___ and P____ are used to it

The next day after lunch
I remember to acknowledge this event
to reassure everyone
R _____ says he is often sick
after strong medication
I love him for this
and all of male company
for their ability to live in chaos
apply logic
condense everything to a
reasoned nugget

Winding along the Dorset coast
stopping at Chesil
Eype

and Lyme Regis
the sun shines
like late August
except it is nearly Halloween
and there's still that nagging
shadow
P_____ drives fast
like he wants to get away
and I know he sees *it* too

On the road
I think of a Sam Cooke song
which E_____ sang
verbatim
when we were here last
climbing that hill on Christmas day
the first year
me and my sisters were sober
it was about a woman
from bible days
who always bled
I look to find the song on my iPhone
just as we are passing that same hill

And I say to P_____
Fucking hell
The moon
the tides
the womb
the menstrual cycle
the lunar cycle
my last ever period coinciding with the full moon

Clover Peake

Moonfleet
The lagoon
a song about a woman who could probably do with a hysterectomy
my brother sang this song at this very spot 10 years ago
I'm gonna have a hysterectomy
it all synchronises
in an absolutely beautiful
poetic way
that is probably
as meaningful as
the handbrake
between us
right now
but there's something in it for me
there has to be
and maybe nothing for you
but I love you so much

Then several days back in London
I can't stop vomiting
on the night before Guy Fawkes
after handing a script to
L_____
paying E_____
recording with G_____
dropping 3 dresses to L_____
I tear the fentanyl patch from my arm
without knowing the withdrawal waiting
and what that fucking
shadow was

Zennor

I wish I was like you
roaring without sense
rolling your back to an arch
to bellow from your guts
unhinging your jaw as you roar
seaweed swinging with the force
you spit at passers-by
crashing against the rocks
time and time again
the same rocks
the ones with crooked faces
to match every loss
with jagged comfort
you roll up
rolling and rolling
unleashing noise into the sky
The birds
hungry for pickings
flinch backwards
passers-by hang back on dry sand
but you persist
scooping shingle to your chest
curling back to shovel your face over the dirt
pummelling the bed with your fists
groaning no words
groans that soften to a whimper
before settling to a billowing sheet of gold

River Crossing

We don't know
I know
only snapshots
in love

We assume

Hell is not hot
but cold
like Valentine's
in the cast-iron bed
curtains closed but sunlight
pushing at the sternum

I leant back against the bedstead
the metal was dark ice
exhaling mist

Dies noctis

Later I walked to the Thames
sat on a bench
before crossing

Maybe back in that room my heart stopped
Yew tree roots burrowed deep

Yesterday we crossed from St Paul's
You gave me jasmine

to bind my wrists
and promised to do all the cooking

Of course I fell in love

From the river bank
I headed to St Charles alone
Waited through the night
under strip lights

My mobile lay by my right hand
you knew where I was
From from there we lost touch

Winter held its breath
Spring laid low

In the garden
the silver sky hid the feint light
barely significant petals
from the Japanese Maple
carried the weight of mercy
effortlessly

The sisters
showed me
my knuckles
could signify a decan

They made that small journey
to tell me
it was understandable

The Blood

The blood
down there
it made me first feel grown up
and then young
First I felt old
then when I was old
it made me feel young again
it made me feel old
it made me feel young
At first I am old
then I am young
In the dark I looked for you
you weren't there
It made me old
then young again
I'm old
then young again
I'm old
I'm young
I'm old
I'm young
I'm old I'm young
I'm old now
I was young then
I'm young now
I was old then
I bled
I don't bleed now
I didn't bleed
I bleed

I'm old
I'm young
I bled
I don't bleed
now

www.ingramcontent.com/pod-product-compliance
Lightning Source LLC
Chambersburg PA
CBHW031509040426
42444CB00007B/1267